The World of
WHALES

BLUE WHALES
GRAY WHALES
KILLER WHALES
HUMPBACK WHALES
FIN WHALES
NARWHALS

Written by Sarah Palmer

Illustrated by David Palmer, Tony Gibbon,
and Sally Hadler

DERRYDALE BOOKS
New York

Originally published in six separate volumes under the titles:
Blue Whales, copyright © 1988 Rourke Enterprises, Inc.
Gray Whales, copyright © 1988 Rourke Enterprises, Inc.
Killer Whales, copyright © 1988 Rourke Enterprises, Inc.
Humpback Whales, copyright © 1988 Rourke Enterprises, Inc.
Fin Whales, copyright © 1988 Rourke Enterprises, Inc.
Narwhals, copyright © 1988 Rourke Enterprises, Inc.
This 1990 edition is published by Derrydale Books,
distributed by Outlet Book Company, Inc., a Random House Company,
225 Park Avenue South, New York, New York 10003, by arrangement
with Rourke Enterprises, Inc.

Printed and bound in the United States of America

Library of Congress Cataloging-in-Publication Data

Palmer, Sarah, 1955–
      World of whales / by Sarah Palmer.
           p.   cm.
      Originally published in six separate vols. as Narwhals, Fin
whales, Blue whales, Killer whales, Humpback whales, Gray whales.
      Summary: Describes the physical characteristics, habitat, and
behavior of six different kinds of whales.
      ISBN 0-517-02746-1
      1. Whales—Juvenile literature.   [1. Whales.]   I. Title.
QL737.C4P36   1990
599.5—dc20
                                                      90-3720
                                                        CIP
                                                        AC

8 7 6 5 4 3 2 1

TABLE OF CONTENTS

BLUE WHALES

BLUE WHALES

Blue whales are baleen whales which do not have any teeth. They take water containing tiny shrimp-like creatures in through the front of their mouth. Then the whales push the water back out into the ocean through the side of their mouth. The **baleen plates** in the side of the blue whale's mouth act like a strainer. They let the water out and keep the food in the whale's mouth.

Blue whales are the largest animals in the world

HOW THEY LOOK

Blue whales are the largest animals ever known. They are even bigger than most of the biggest dinosaurs. Blue whales can grow as long as 100 feet. Some weigh almost 160 tons. A full-grown blue whale has over 300 baleen plates on each side of his mouth. Blue whales have a dark, slate-blue back, with light colored flecks. The underside is pale.

A blue whale blows at the surface of the ocean

WHERE THEY LIVE

Blue whales can be found in three different places. Some live in the Antarctic Ocean. Others live in the North Atlantic and North Pacific Oceans. In the winter, blue whales **migrate** to warmer waters. They eat very little during their stay in warm waters. Blue whales are always the first whales to return to the cold **polar** waters in the spring. There they always find a lot to eat.

Blue whales spend half the year in cold, polar oceans

WHAT THEY EAT

Like all baleen whales, blue whales live mainly on small shrimp-like creatures called **krill**. The krill is taken in with water from the ocean. It is swallowed after the whale has strained the water out from his mouth through the baleen plates. Blue whales eat a ton of krill in one mouthful. They are so big that they have to eat many tons of food each day.

Blue whales eat small creatures called krill

Today it is unusual to see more than three blue whales together

Blue whales are baleen whales

LIVING IN THE OCEAN

Much of the blue whales' time is spent feeding. The whales that live in the Antarctic Ocean grow bigger than the ones found in the northern oceans. Scientists believe there may be more food for the whales in the Antarctic Ocean. The food may also be richer in **vitamins**. The blue whales that live in the north have separate lives from those in the south. They never meet, even when both groups migrate to warmer waters.

Blue whales eat tons of krill and plankton each day

BABY BLUE WHALES

Blue whales are as big as some full-grown whales when they are born. An average blue whale **calf** is 23 feet long and weighs over 5 tons at birth. Calves drink only their mothers' milk for the first six months of their life. The milk is rich in vitamins and the calf grows very quickly. Blue whale calves grow a surprising 2 inches and 200 pounds each day during this time.

Baby blue whales grow very quickly

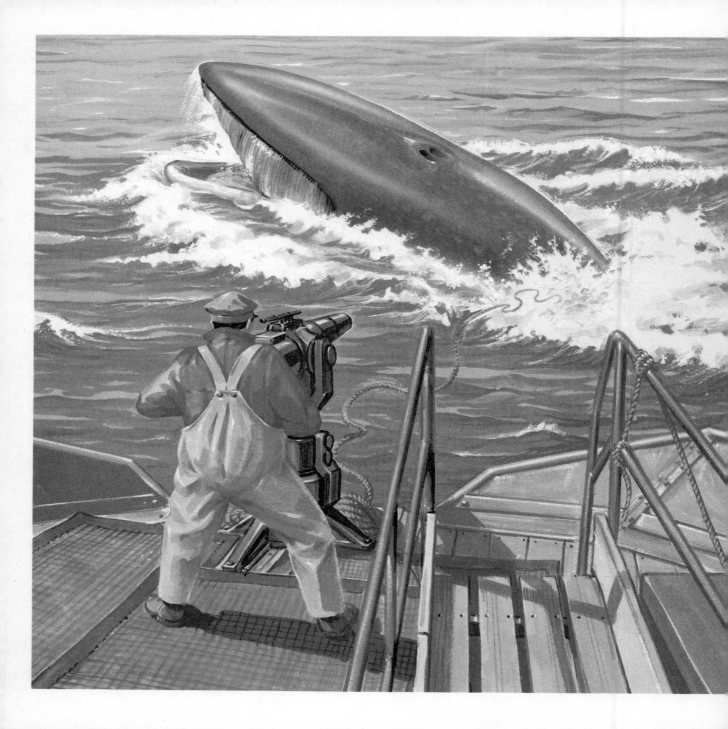

BLUE WHALES AND PEOPLE

Whales used to be hunted with a harpoon, a kind of spear attached to a rope. The **whalers** threw the harpoon at the whale and anchored it in its skin. But blue whales are so strong that they easily pulled away. Not many blue whales were caught in the early days of whaling. When the whalers began to use the **harpoon gun** in 1868, even the blue whales could no longer escape.

A whaler shoots a blue whale with a harpoon gun

SAVING BLUE WHALES

Blue whales were prized for their **blubber**. This thick layer of fat under the skin was boiled down to make **blubber oil**, also called **whale oil**. Blue whales have more blubber than most whales. The blubber from an average blue whale makes between 10 and 20 tons of oil. The most oil ever made from a blue whale was 50 tons. So many blue whales were killed by whalers that very few are left. Now no one is allowed to kill blue whales.

Blue whales were the whalers' favorite whales

FACT FILE

Common Name:	Blue Whale
Scientific Name:	Balaenoptera musculus
Type:	Baleen whale
Color:	Dark slate-blue
Size:	up to 100 feet
Weight:	up to 155 tons
Number in World:	14,000

GRAY WHALES

GRAY WHALES

Gray whales are very ugly. Their skin is covered in warts and pimples and is crusted with **barnacles**. You may have seen barnacles on the bottom of boats. Like humpback whales, gray whales suffer from **parasites** such as whale-lice. The whale-lice attach themselves to the whales' skin and feed on their blood.

Skin parasites make gray whales look ugly

HOW THEY LOOK

Gray whales may look strange, but their movements are very graceful. They are beautiful to watch as they swim. They twist and turn under the water with great ease. The medium-sized gray whales are about 45 feet long. They weigh around 20 tons. The female gray whales are larger than the males. Gray whales have no **dorsal fin** on their backs.

Gray whales are very graceful

WHERE THEY LIVE

Gray whales live in the North Pacific Ocean during the summer months. They like the freezing waters in the far north. Many gray whales live in the Beaufort Sea, north of Canada and Alaska. During the winter, some gray whales **migrate** down the west coast of the United States to California. Others travel towards Japan to the Sea of Okhotsk.

Gray whales like the freezing waters of the far north

WHAT THEY EAT

Like all **baleen** whales, gray whales eat small shrimp-like creatures called **krill**, and tiny plants known as **plankton**. The northern seas where they live are very rich with this food. The whales spend the summers eating huge amounts of krill and plankton. This builds up their thick layer of fat, or **blubber**, which keeps the whales warm. In winter the whales do not eat very much at all.

Gray whales use their baleen plates when feeding

Gray whales can grow to about 45 feet long

Gray whales have a thick layer of blubber

LIVING IN THE OCEAN

The gray whales' main enemies in the oceans are the cruel killer whales. These two whales follow the same migration route along the coast of California. The killer whales normally feed on salmon and other large fish. Sometimes they attack the gray whales. Killer whales are smaller than gray whales, but their huge teeth give them the advantage.

Killer whales sometimes attack gray whales

BABY GRAY WHALES

Baby gray whales are born in the winter. At that time the gray whales are living in the oceans off California. The mother swims to shallow water close to land. There the **calf** is born in the warm and sheltered water. At birth the calf weighs well over a ton. It is 16 feet long. Many people travel to California to see the gray whales with their babies.

Baby gray whales are born in warm lagoons

GRAY WHALES AND PEOPLE

Female gray whales keep a very close watch on their calves. If people come too close, the mother gray whale takes action. She rams the boat to warn humans to stay away from her calf. But not even mother gray whales stopped the **whalers**. They killed hundreds of gray whales in the Californian **lagoons**.

Many people come to watch the gray whales and their calves

SAVING GRAY WHALES

The whalers found gray whales very easy to catch. They waited for them to come to the coast of California. There they could round up the mother and baby gray whales very quickly. At one time, people thought that there were no gray whales left. Then some were seen in California, and the whalers were forbidden to kill them. Now there are more than 6,000 gray whales in our oceans.

Whalers found gray whales very easy to catch in the lagoons

FACT FILE

Common Name:	Gray Whale
Scientific Name:	Eschrichtius robustus
Type:	Baleen whale
Color:	Gray
Size:	average 45 feet
Weight:	up to 20 tons
Number in World:	18,000

KILLER WHALES

KILLER WHALES

Killer whales are **toothed whales**, which means that they have teeth to eat fish and meat. Not all whales have teeth. Killer whales have teeth that fit tightly together and are very strong. They are called killer whales because their powerful jaws and teeth allow them to eat other animals. Sometimes killer whales eat whales even larger than themselves.

Killer whales have powerful jaws and teeth

HOW THEY LOOK

Killer whales are black with large white markings on their undersides and on the side of the head. Killer whales have the longest **dorsal fin** of any whale. The dorsal fin of the male can be as long as 6 feet. Killer whales are medium-sized whales. The male grows to an average of 30 feet long and the female is about 18 feet long. A male killer whale usually weighs around 9 tons.

Male killer whales have very long dorsal fins

WHERE THEY LIVE

Killer whales live in the cold waters of the northern Pacific and Atlantic Oceans. They are often seen off the western coast of North America, near Alaska and British Columbia. Killer whales also live south of Africa and Australia in the cold **Antarctic** seas. In the winter, families of killer whales **migrate** to warmer waters. That's where the young are born.

Killer whales like cold water

WHAT THEY EAT

Killer whales are fun to watch, but they can be very deadly. As few as five and sometimes as many as fifty killer whales hunt together in packs. They attack all kinds of fish. They also eat other animals, like seals and penguins, that are found in the icy regions where the whales live. If a killer whale sees a seal sitting on an **ice floe**, he may ram his body against it to make the seal fall off. He then eats the seal.

Killer whales sometimes eat seals

Killer whales are usually found in
groups

Killer whales have beautiful black
and white markings

LIVING IN THE OCEAN

All whales are **mammals**, and they need air to breathe. They cannot breathe underwater. Killer whales come to the surface of the water to breathe. They breathe through a hole in the top of their head, which is known as a **blowhole**. The whales keep their blowhole closed while they are underwater. They open it when they want to breathe in and out at the surface.

Killer whales breathe through blowholes

BABY KILLER WHALES

At the end of the summer the killer whale family has completed the long **migration** from cold to warm waters. They may have journeyed from Alaska past the coast of California to Mexico. The killer whale **calves** are born while the family is in warm waters. At birth the baby whale has the same patterned markings as its parents. The patches are yellow, but they turn white as the calf grows up. The killer whale calf stays close to its mother for the first year of his life. It is very playful.

Killer whale calves stay close to their mothers

KILLER WHALES AND PEOPLE

Killer whales can be seen in many marine parks and zoos in the United States. These whales are members of the dolphin family and perform similar tricks. They leap right out the water. Sometimes killer whales like to stand on their tails with their heads out of the water. Although killer whales are cruel to other animals in the ocean, they are very gentle and playful in the marine parks.

Killer whales are fun to watch at the marine park

SAVING KILLER WHALES

No creatures in the ocean dare to threaten the fierce killer whales. Their only **predators** are man. Killer whales are hunted and captured for marine parks. They are popular because they learn different tricks very fast and are fun to watch. So many killer whales have been captured for zoos that for a while many people worried that none would be left in the ocean. Today you must have a permit to take killer whales from the ocean.

Many killer whales were caught for zoos

FACT FILE

Common Name:	Killer Whale, Orca
Scientific Name:	Orcinus orca
Type:	Toothed whale
Color:	Black with white patches
Size:	up to 30 feet
Weight:	up to 10 tons
Number in World:	Scientists have not counted how many killer whales live in the oceans. They are thought to be plentiful.

HUMPBACK WHALES

HUMPBACK WHALES

Humpback whales are often seen leaping from the water. This is called **breaching**. They look happy, but humpbacks are always itchy. They suffer from **parasites** that live on their skin and tickle them. When the humpback whales breach, they slap themselves hard down on the water. It looks as if they are trying to shake the parasites off their skin.

Humpback whales are often seen breaching

HOW THEY LOOK

Humpback whales have the longest flippers of any whale. Their flippers are about 14 feet long and have a bumpy front edge. The skin of the humpback whales is dark along their back. They are white underneath and under their long flippers. Humpback whales can grow up to 60 feet long. An average humpback weighs over 40 tons.

Humpback whales have very long, bumpy flippers

WHERE THEY LIVE

Humpback whales live in the North Atlantic and North Pacific Oceans. Humpbacks **migrate** to warmer waters in the cold winter months. It takes them three months to reach their new homes in Bermuda or the Hawaiian Islands. Humpbacks always migrate to exactly the same place each year. They defend their right to that **territory**. Humpback whales are often seen close to shore.

*Humpback whales often swim
close to shore*

WHAT THEY EAT

Humpback whales eat small fish and tiny plants called **plankton**. This food is strained through the whale bones in their cheeks. These bones are called **baleen plates**. Humpback whales herd schools of fish into a tight group. This way they can get many fish into their mouths in one try. Sometimes seabirds peck at the schools of fish the whales have rounded up. If they are not careful, they also get swallowed by the humpbacks!

Humpback whales feed on tiny fish and plants

Humpback whales suffer from skin parasites

The songs of the humpback whales are very beautiful

LIVING IN THE OCEAN

Whales talk to each other underwater. They use a series of clicks and whistles. These noises are also used to help the whales find their way. The echoes from the sounds the whales make are bounced off objects in the water. The whale can tell from the echo what the objects are. Sometimes the sounds whales make are like singing. The beautiful ''songs'' of the humpback whales are very famous.

Humpback whales can "talk" to each other underwater

BABY HUMPBACK WHALES

Newborn humpback whales, called **calves**, do not have any **blubber**. Blubber is the thick layer of fat under the whales' skin. It keeps the whales warm in the freezing oceans. Humpback calves would not survive if they were born in the cold northern seas. They are born after the family has migrated to warmer waters for the winter. The baby humpback is a darker color than its parents.

Baby humpbacks are darker gray than their parents

HUMPBACK WHALES AND PEOPLE

Humpback whales were hunted for their baleen plates or whale bone. These plates are very strong and quite **flexible**. Whale bone was used for fashionable ladies' corsets. The bristles on the baleen plates also had many uses. They were used for making wigs and for stuffing furniture. The blubber of humpback whales was used for making oil.

Humpback whales were hunted for their baleen plates

SAVING HUMPBACK WHALES

Humpback whales are slow swimmers. They like to swim close to shore. This made humpbacks easy **prey** for the **whalers**. In the early part of this century there were very few humpback whales left in the oceans. The whalers had killed nearly all of them. No one is allowed to kill humpback whales anymore. Scientists believe there are about 10,000 humpbacks left in the world.

Humpback whales were easy prey for the whalers

FACT FILE

Common Name:	Humpback Whale
Scientific Name:	Megaptera novaeangliae
Type:	Baleen whale
Color:	Gray
Size:	up to 60 feet
Weight:	up to 40 tons
Number in World:	10,000

FIN WHALES

FIN WHALES

The fin whale is the world's most common whale. It is also known as the ''common rorqual.'' Fin whales are **baleen whales**. They have no teeth, and they trap food in their mouth using **baleen plates**. Fin whales can swim very fast. A close relative of the fin whale is the **Sei whale**. Sei whales look like fin whales but are smaller.

Sei whales are like small fin whales

HOW THEY LOOK

Fin whales have a dark gray or brownish back and a pure white underside. They are medium-sized whales. Fin whales can grow up to 80 feet long and normally weigh about 65 tons. Very long **grooves** run right down their underside. These grooves are actually folds in the fin whales' skin. When the whales take in food and water, the folds stretch out so they can hold more in their mouth and throat.

90

Fin whales have long grooves right down their undersides

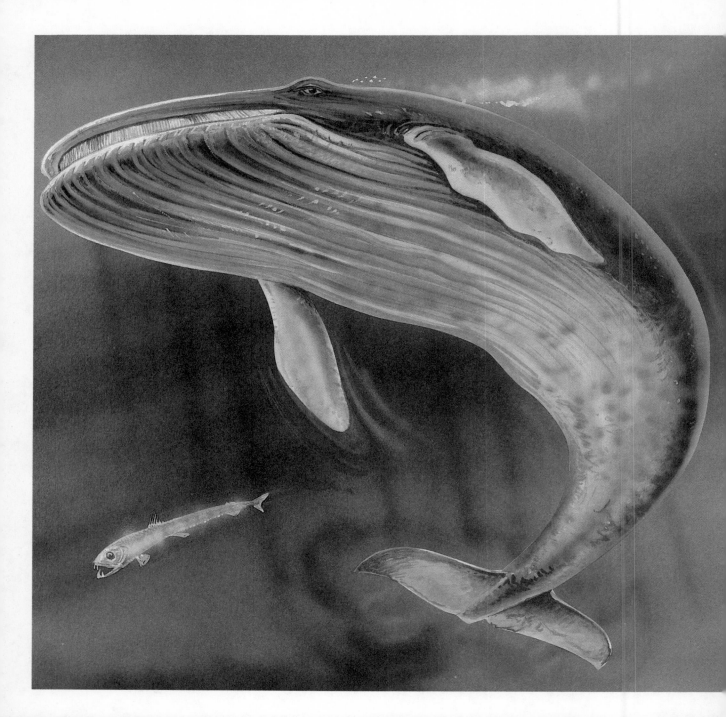

WHERE THEY LIVE

Like other types of whales, fin whales are separated into two groups. One group lives in the north. Fin whales have been seen off Alaska and Canada, and even as far north as Greenland. The other group of fin whales lives in the southern oceans toward the South Pole. Most of the time fin whales like to live in deep water. Sometimes they come close to land.

Fin whales like to live in deep,
cold water

WHAT THEY EAT

Herring, a kind of fish, is the fin whales' favorite food. Fin whales have been watched hunting herrings. They swim around the herrings to push them together into a tight group. The fish see only the fin whale's pure white underside flashing past them. They are stunned by the quick movement and bright light. When the whale has herded the herrings close together, he opens up his great mouth and swallows them.

Herring are the fin whales'
favorite food

Fin whales can swim very fast

Fin whales dive deep into the ocean

LIVING IN THE OCEAN

Fin whales like to live in deep water. Sometimes they dive deep into the water. They can stay underwater for up to an hour. Usually they stay under much less time than that. The whales come back to the surface of the water to breathe air. Sometimes they **spout** when they come back up. A fin whale's spout is more than 15 feet high.

98

A fin whale's spout can be over 15 feet high

BABY FIN WHALES

The fin whale parents have a baby, or **calf**, every two years. Like most other whales, the fin whale calves are born during the winter when the family is in warmer waters closer to the **equator**. The fin whale calf is 22 feet long at birth. It can weigh as much as 4½ tons. Young fin whales stay close to their mothers for the first twelve months of their lives.

Baby fin whales are born in warm water

FIN WHALES AND PEOPLE

Fin whales have been one of the most hunted whales. When blue whales became rare, the **whalers** started to hunt fin whales. The whalers called the fin whales "razorbacks" because they have a long ridge down their back. The whalers could catch several fin whales at once, because the whales all stayed together to help each other.

Fin whales have a long ridge down their back

SAVING FIN WHALES

Fin whales have thick **blubber** to protect them from the cold. The blubber from one fin whale can make up to 8 tons of oil. Earlier in this century the whalers were killing 10,000 fin whales each year. They used the blubber for oil and the baleen plates or whale bone for corsets. Today fin whales are protected by law. Whalers can no longer kill them.

A large fin whale could upset a small ship

FACT FILE

Common Name:	Fin Whale, Common Rorqual
Scientific Name:	Balaenoptera physalus
Type:	Baleen whale
Color:	Dark gray or brown
Size:	up to 80 feet
Weight:	average 65 tons
Number in World:	120,000

NARWHALS

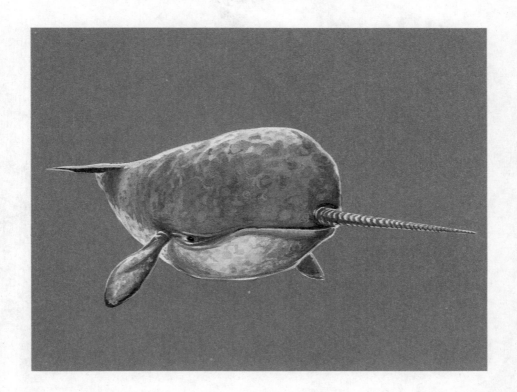

NARWHALS

Narwhals are very easy to recognize. Male narwhals have a long **tusk** which grows from one side of the mouth. Imagine that your top left front tooth is growing outward in front of you. That is where the narwhal's tusk grows from. Narwhals are **toothed whales**.

Male narwhals can grow up to 18 feet long

HOW THEY LOOK

Narwhals are quite small whales. They rarely weigh more than a ton. Narwhals can grow up to 18 feet long. The tusk of the male narwhal is usually about 6 to 9 feet long. Female narwhals do not have a tusk. Narwhals are pale brown with darker brown spots on their backs. They do not have a **dorsal fin**.

Female narwhals do not have tusks

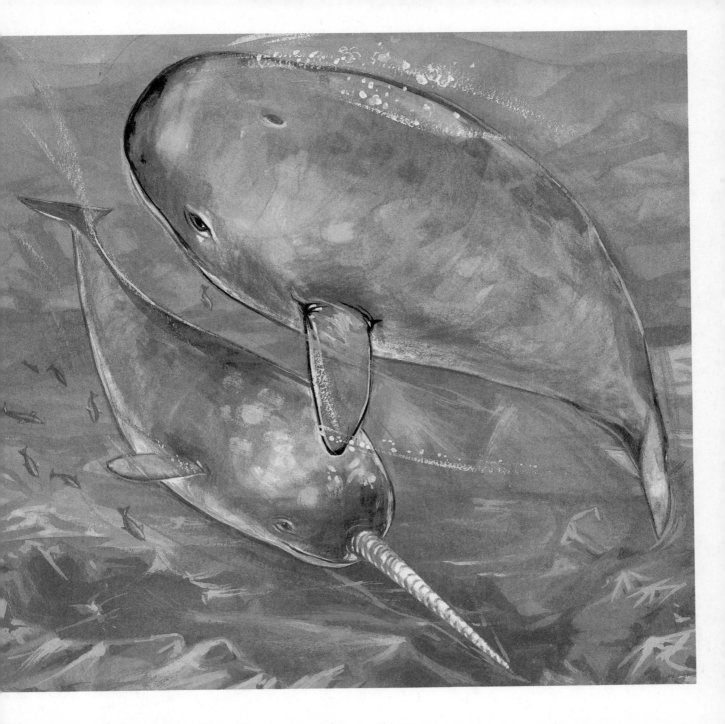

WHERE THEY LIVE

Narwhals live in the Arctic Ocean east of Canada. They like very cold temperatures. Narwhals remain in the Arctic seas year-round. They do not **migrate** to warmer seas during the winter. As the ice melts in the summer, the narwhals move farther north into the Arctic. They like to dive right under the ice. When the narwhals need to breathe, they come up through holes in the ice.

Narwhals live in the cold Arctic Ocean

WHAT THEY EAT

Narwhals are toothed whales. Toothed whales are able to grip large creatures in their teeth. Narwhals eat cod and other large fish. They also eat squid, cuttlefish, and **crustaceans** such as shrimp. The male narwhal's long tusk does not seem to get in the way when he hunts.

Narwhals eat fish and crustaceans

Narwhals are some of the
smallest whales

Narwhals do not have dorsal fins

LIVING IN THE OCEAN

Narwhals share their cold home with a variety of Arctic creatures. While they feed on the many fish, the narwhals are **prey** for some of the larger animals. Sometimes the tusk of the male narwhal will give away his hiding place under the ice. He may be spotted by a polar bear. The hungry bear will attack and eat the narwhal.

Polar bears are known to attack narwhals

BABY NARWHALS

The narwhals' mating season is in April. The narwhal **calves** are born in July or August the following year. They are born with only a thin layer of **blubber** or fat, one inch thick. As the young narwhals grow, their blubber becomes thicker. Narwhal calves remain close to their mothers for eighteen months.

Narwhal calves stay very close to their mothers

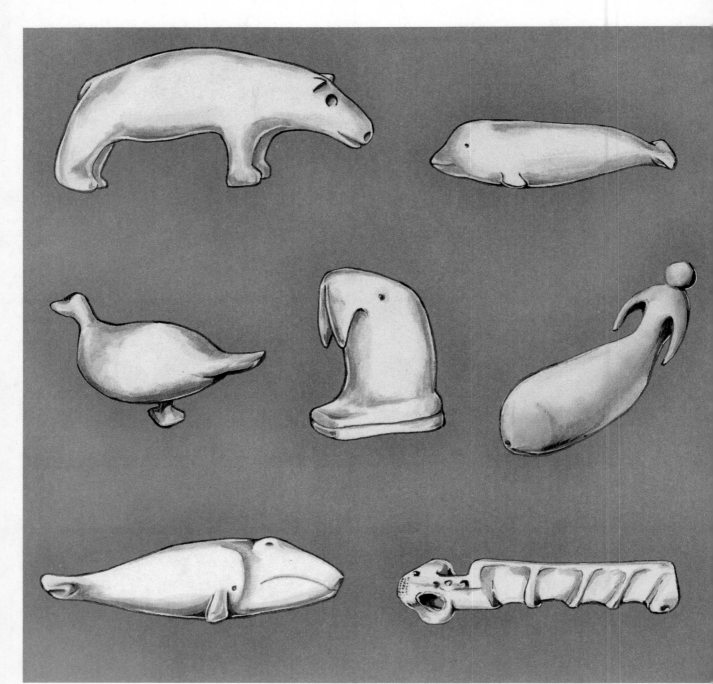

NARWHALS AND PEOPLE

Narwhals have always been highly prized by people. Eskimos hunt narwhals for their tusks. Like elephants' tusks, narwhal tusks are made of **ivory**. With their delicately spiraled pattern, narwhal tusks can be carved into beautiful ornaments. The Chinese believe that narwhal tusks have special powers. They use them to make medicine.

123

Narwhals' tusks are made of ivory

SAVING THE NARWHAL

There are probably about 30,000 narwhals left in the world. They are only found in the Arctic. Narwhals have been heavily hunted by the Eskimos. The Eskimos use every part of a narwhal. They eat the meat and use the blubber for oil. The skin is very rich in **vitamins** and has a delicious sweet taste. The Eskimos eat narwhal skin raw. They kill about 500 narwhals each year.

Narwhal meat is very rich in vitamins

FACT FILE

Common Name:	Narwhal
Scientific Name:	Monodon monoceros
Type:	Toothed whale
Color:	Pale brown with dark markings
Size:	up to 18 feet
Weight:	up to 1 ton
Number in World:	about 30,000

GLOSSARY

Antarctic (and ARC tic)—the area around the South Pole

baleen plates (BAL een PLATES)—whalebones used to strain food in a whale's mouth

barnacles (BAR nac les)—small animals with hard shells that attach themselves to rocks, boats or whales

blowhole (BLOW HOLE)—a nostril located on top of a whale's head

blubber (BLUB ber)—a thick layer of fat under a whale's skin

crustaceans (crust A ceans)—sea animals with hard shells such as crabs and lobsters

dorsal fin (DOR sal FIN)—a fin on a whale's back

harpoon gun (har POON GUN)—a spear-gun used in hunting whales

ice floe (ICE FLOE)—a sheet of floating ice

krill (KRILL)—tiny shrimp-like creatures on which whales feed

lagoons (la GOONS)—shallow bays

migration (mi GRA tion)—the movement from one place to another, usually at the same time each year

parasites (PAR a sites)—animals that depend on others for food without giving anything in return

plankton (PLANK ton)—tiny plants on which whales feed

predators (PRED a tors)—animals that hunt others for food

territory (TER ri tor y)—a claimed area of land or sea

to breach (BREACH)—to leap clear of the water

to spout (SPOUT)—to breathe out a mixture of air and water high into the air

tusk (TUSK)—a long, pointed tooth which sticks out from the mouth

whalers (WHAL ers)—people who hunt whales